String Companions

Duet Collection
(For Violin and Viola Duet)

Compiled, Arranged, and Edited
by HARVEY S. WHISTLER and HERMAN A. HUMMEL

RUBANK®

HAL•LEONARD®
CORPORATION

7777 W. BLUEMOUND RD. P.O. BOX 13819 MILWAUKEE, WI 53213

Duo Célèbre

PLEYEL

Duo Chromatic

EICHBERG

Aragonaise

MAZAS

Rondo Scherzando

BRUNI

La Fileuse

ALARD

1349-31

La Champétre

MAZAS

Duo de Masqué

DANCLA

Scherzo - Caprice

GEBAUER

Morceau Lyrique

DANCLA

Pièce de Concert

DANCLA

Rondo Brillante

GEBAUER

Duo Dramatique

JANSA

Salon-Duett

HOHMANN

Polka de Concert

DANCLA

Duettino in F

DANCLA

La Chasse

HOFFMEISTER

Elfentanz

EICHBERG

Sizelietta

CAMPAGNOLI

1349-31

Canzonetta

BÖHM

Rondo Allegro
from the Grand Duo de Concert

SPOHR

Concertstück

KALLIWODA

1349-31

Duo Concertante

VIOTTI

Duo Symphonique

CAMPAGNOLI

Folies d' Espagne
(Theme and Variations)

CORELLI

Theme and Variation
on the Air "Barucaba"

PAGANINI